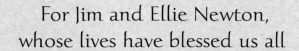

For Jim and Ellie Newton,
whose lives have blessed us all

*I am deeply grateful to the following family members, friends,
colleagues, and other extremely helpful contributors for their time,
energy, knowledge, and expertise, and above all for their continuing
thoughtful support and encouragement of this project.
It made all the difference.*

Wendy Boase; Laura, David, and Bea Brody; Elizabeth and Susannah Brown;
David Buchdahl; Priscilla Wardwell Carlebach; Edie Ching; Susan Cooper;
Margaret N. Coughlin; Caroline DeMaio; Beth Dugger; Brian Dunne; Amy
Ehrlich; Connie Feydy; Carol Fox; The Franciscan Center in Little Falls,
Minnesota; Florence Goldberg; Rachel Hadas; Ben and Rosalie Harris; Saran M.
Hutchins; Lucy Ingrams; Anne Irza-Leggat; Julius Lester; Anne Morrow Lindbergh;
Anne Spencer Lindbergh; Sarah, Brian, and Scott Lindbergh; Raquel Milano;
Stephen Mitchell; Anne Moore; James D. and Eleanor F. Newton; Elizabeth
O'Donnell; Katherine Paterson; Noel Perrin; Gale Pryor; Meg Raftis and
Madeleine L'Engle; Lisa Riley; Caroline Royds; Marek Sapieyevski; the Sheerin
family; Catherine Soares; David Sterling; Alice W. Tripp; Nat, Eli, Sam, and Ben
Tripp; Liz Truslow; Janna Weiss (and Agam!); Kevin and Marlene White

~ R. L. ~

Introduction and this selection copyright © 2000 by Reeve Lindbergh
Text copyright © year of publication by individual authors as noted in Acknowledgments
Illustrations in For the Day copyright © 2000 by Bob Graham
Illustrations in For the Home copyright © 2000 by Elisa Kleven
Illustrations in For the Earth copyright © 2000 by Christine Davenier
Illustrations in For the Night copyright © 2000 by Anita Jeram

First edition 2000

Library of Congress Cataloging-in-Publication Data is available.

Library of Congress Catalog Card Number 99-089379

ISBN 0-7636-0176-4

2 4 6 8 10 9 7 5 3

Printed in Hong Kong

Bob Graham's illustrations were done in watercolor and ink; Elisa Kleven's in watercolor and collage;
Christine Davenier's in watercolor; and Anita Jeram's in acrylic.
This book was typeset in Kosmik, Oxalis, and Tapioca.

*A portion of the author's royalties from this book will go to Ocean Arks International,
working toward clean water for the health of children everywhere.*

Candlewick Press, 2067 Massachusetts Avenue, Cambridge, Massachusetts 02140

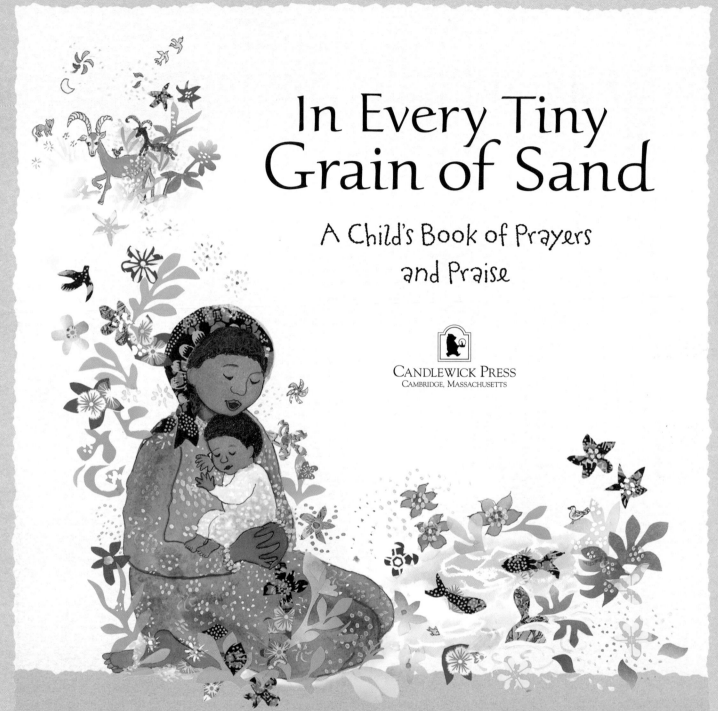

In Every Tiny Grain of Sand

A Child's Book of Prayers and Praise

CANDLEWICK PRESS
CAMBRIDGE, MASSACHUSETTS

COLLECTED BY Reeve Lindbergh

ILLUSTRATED BY

Christine Davenier, Bob Graham, Anita Jeram, and Elisa Kleven

 *In Every Tiny Grain of Sand* is a collection of prayers and poems and other writings, gathered from many different sources. Some of them were written in appreciation of nature, or to praise God, or to celebrate good things in our lives like our families, our homes, and our love for one another. Others were written when the writer needed strength, comfort, or courage. The words in this collection were written by many different people, of all ages, cultures, and religions from all over the world. Some were written in ancient times, others just a few years ago.

I have known and loved some of these pieces since I was very young, like my favorite Robert Browning poem, "Pippa's Song," which ends with these lines: "The lark's on the wing; / The snail's on the thorn; / God's in his heaven—/ All's right with the world!"

This poem has always given me a joyful sense of the beauty of nature and the presence of God all around us. I also liked to read the Twenty-third Psalm from the Bible quietly to myself when I was troubled or afraid. I would try to imagine lying down in "green pastures," beside "still waters." Those words always made me feel better.

Some poems and prayers became familiar to me because my family knew and loved them. It was my mother, a lifelong writer, poet, and bird-lover, who told me that Pope Pius XII once said, "Feeding the birds is also a form of prayer." My sister Anne, another poet and writer, memorized Gerard Manley Hopkins's poem "Pied Beauty" and recited it to me. "'Glory be to God for dappled things—'" she would begin, "'For skies of couple-color as a brinded cow'. . ." I still don't know what a brinded cow is, exactly, but I can feel the glory of creation, in a simple way that makes sense, whenever I read that poem.

After I grew up, I learned that other people loved the same kinds of poems and prayers that meant so much to my family and me. When I was putting this book together, I wrote to my family and my friends, and then to people I didn't even know, all over the world, asking them to send me their favorite poems and prayers. Many, many people responded, and with their help, *In Every Tiny Grain of Sand* came into being.

This is a book to share with your family, or to read all by yourself. You can read it at special times, or at any time. It is arranged in four sections: For the Day, For the Home, For the Earth, and For the Night, but you can also just look through it to find the prayers and poems that mean the most to you. However you choose to use this book, I hope the poems and prayers in it will bring to you, as they have brought to me, much joy, and strength, and comfort, and many other blessings.

Reeve Lindbergh

Contents

For the Day

illustrated by BOB GRAHAM

This is the day that the Lord hath made:
let us rejoice and be glad in it

I am like a bear.
I hold up my hands
waiting for the sun to rise.

Pawnee

O Mother, you are light and your light is everywhere.
Streaming from your body are rays in thousands—
two thousand, a hundred thousand,
tens of millions, a hundred million—
there is no counting their numbers.
It is by you and through you that all things moving
and motionless shine. It is by your light,
O Mother, that all things come to be.

from the BHAIRAVA YAMALA
Hindu

10

Thank You, God of everything,
for the morning,
when I wake again
to You.

Jewish

May the Lord bless you and protect you.
May the Lord show you kindness and be gracious to you.
May the Lord bestow favor upon you and grant you peace.

Jewish

O God, give me, I pray Thee,
light on my right hand
and light on my left hand
and light above me
and light beneath me,
O Lord, increase light within me
and give me light
and illuminate me.

Muslim

Do harm to nobody;
Pray for all;
Try to make your light shine in the world
And let your banner fly high
In the Heavens.

Baha'i

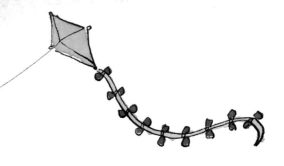

PIPPA'S SONG

The year's at the spring;
And day's at the morn;
Morning's at seven;
The hill-side's dew-pearled;
The lark's on the wing;
The snail's on the thorn;
God's in his heaven—
All's right with the world!

ROBERT BROWNING

13

May the blessing of light
be on you, light without and light within.

May the blessed sunlight
shine upon you and warm your heart till it glows
like a great peat fire, so that the stranger may
come and warm himself at it, as well as the friend.
And may the light shine out of the eyes of you,
like a candle set in the windows of a house,
bidding the wanderer to come in out of the storm.

And may the blessing of the rain
be on you—the soft sweet rain.
May it fall upon your spirit so that all the little flowers may spring up,
and shed their sweetness on the air.
And may the blessing of the great rains be on you,
that they beat upon your spirit and wash it fair and clean,
and leave there many a shining pool where the blue
of heaven shines, and sometimes a star.

And may the blessing of the earth
be on you—the great round earth;
may you ever have a kindly greeting
for people you pass as you are going along the roads.

And now may the Lord
bless you, and bless you kindly.

Celtic

14

O Lord, my God,
I pray that these things never end:
The sand and the sea,
The rush of the waters,
The crash of the heavens,
The prayer of the heart.
The sand and the sea,
The rush of the waters,
The crash of the heavens,
The prayer of the heart.

HANNAH SENESH

16

Supreme Lord, let there be peace in the sky.
And in the atmosphere,
Peace in the plant world and in the forests;
Let the cosmic powers be peaceful;
Let Brahma be peaceful;
Let there be undiluted and fulfilling peace
everywhere.

Hindu

Master of the Universe,
Grant me the ability to be alone;
May it be my custom to go outdoors each day
Among the trees and grasses,
Among all growing things,
And there may I be alone,
And enter into prayer
To talk with the one
That I belong to.

RABBI NACHMAN OF BRATSLAV

This is the day that the Lord hath made:
let us rejoice and be glad in it!

from Psalm 118

Turn,
Trust God,
Fling from thee all that is less.

GURU NANAK

The flute of the Infinite is played without ceasing, and its sound is love.

KABIR

The Lord is my shepherd; I shall not want.

He maketh me to lie down in green pastures:
    he leadeth me beside the still waters.

He restoreth my soul: he leadeth me in the paths
    of righteousness for his name's sake.

Yea, though I walk through the valley of the shadow
    of death, I will fear no evil: for thou art with me;
    thy rod and thy staff they comfort me.

Thou preparest a table before me in the presence
    of mine enemies: thou anointest my head with oil;
    my cup runneth over.

Surely goodness and mercy shall follow me all the days
    of my life: and I will dwell in the house
    of the Lord for ever.

Psalm 23

THE CIRCLE OF DAYS

Lord, we offer thanks and praise
  For the circle of our days.

Praise for radiant brother sun
  Who makes the hours around us run.

For sister moon, and for the stars,
  Brilliant, precious, always ours.

Praise for brothers wind and air,
  Serene or cloudy, foul or fair.

For sister water, clear and chaste,
  Useful, humble, good to taste.

For fire, our brother, strong and bright,
  Whose joy illuminates the night.

Praise for our sister, mother earth,
  Who cares for each of us from birth.

For all her children, fierce or mild,
  For sister, brother, parent, child.

For creatures wild and creatures tame,
  For hunter, hunted, both the same.

For brother sleep, and sister death,
  Who tend the borders of our breath.

For desert, orchard, rock, and tree,
  For forest, meadow, mountain, sea,

For fruit and flower, plant and bush,
  For morning robin, evening thrush.

For all your gifts, of every kind,
  We offer praise with quiet mind.

Be with us, Lord, and guide our ways
  Around the circle of our days.

REEVE LINDBERGH
based on CANTICLE OF THE SUN, ST. FRANCIS OF ASSISI

There is a Light that shines
    beyond all things on earth,
    beyond us all,
    beyond the heavens,
    beyond the highest,
    the very highest heavens.
This is the Light that shines in our heart.

from the CHANDOGYA UPANISHAD

May the sun rise well;
    may the earth appear
    brightly shone upon!

May the moon rise well;
    may the earth appear
    brightly shone upon!

Teton Sioux

By day the sun shines,
   and by night shines the moon.
The warrior shines in his armor,
   and the priest in his meditation.
But the Buddha shines
   by day and by night:
In the brightness of his glory
   shines the man who is awake.

from the DHAMMAPADA

25

For the Home

illustrated by ELISA KLEVEN

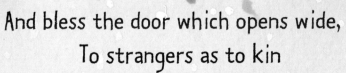
And bless the door which opens wide,
To strangers as to kin

One generation passes away,
   and another generation comes:
But the earth abides forever.
The sun also rises, and the sun goes down,
And hastens to his place where he arose.

The wind goes toward the south,
And turns about unto the north;
It whirls about continually,
And the wind returns again
   according to his circuits.

All the rivers run into the sea;
Yet the sea is not full:
Unto the place whence the rivers come,
There they return again.

from Ecclesiastes

God bless the master of this house, Likewise the mistress too,

And all the little children That round the table go.

Wassail song

30

Bless the four corners of this house,
    And be the lintel blessed,
And bless the hearth and bless the board,
    And bless each place of rest.

And bless the door which opens wide,
    To strangers as to kin,
And bless each crystal window pane
    That lets the sunshine in;

And bless the rooftree overhead,
    And every sturdy wall—
The peace of man, the peace of God,
    The peace of love on all.

Christian

If in your heart you make a manger for his birth,
    then God will once again become a child on earth.

ANGELUS SILESIUS

All shall be well
and all shall be well
and all manner of thing shall be well.

JULIAN OF NORWICH

See the world as your self.
Have faith in the way things are.
Love the world as your self;
Then you can care for all things.

LAO-TZU

God bless all those that I love;
God bless all those that love me:
God bless all those that love those that I love
And all those that love those that love me.

New England sampler

32

May it be delightful my house;
From my head may it be delightful;
To my feet may it be delightful;
Where I lie may it be delightful;
All above me may it be delightful;
All around me may it be delightful.

Navajo

The bread is pure and fresh,
   the water is cool and clear.
Lord of all life, be with us,
   Lord of all life, be near.

African

For every cup and plateful,
   God make us truly grateful.

Christian

Bless this food to our use,
   and us to Thy service. Amen.

Christian

Blessed art thou, O Lord our God,
   King of the universe,
   who brings forth bread
   from the earth.

Jewish

BREAD

Be gentle when you touch Bread.
Let it not lie
Uncared for,
Unwanted.
So often Bread
Is taken for granted.

Beauty of patient toil,
Wind and rain
Have caressed it.
Christ often blessed it.
Be gentle when you touch Bread.

FREDA ELTON YOUNG

MOTHER OF BROWN-NESS

EARTH-MOTHER,

Mother of all our brown-ness,

Hands clasped with arms

stretching round the world,

Cuddle me closer, warm upon your breast

Slumberous, sweetly, darkness at rest.

Wake me to living and loving;

Scatter my dreams into the ethereal air.

Mother of brown-ness surround me

Deep in your sweet loving care.

MARGARET WALKER

The lands around my dwelling
Are more beautiful
From the day
When it is given me to see
Faces I have never seen before.
All is more beautiful,
All is more beautiful,
And life is thankfulness.
These guests of mine
Make my house grand.

Inuit

ALONE

Alone in the peace and cool of the evening,
    we fished the waters of our ancient land
        as birds headed to the havens of their nests,
            and we lived under the gentleness
                of Biami's hand.

BUDGER DAVISON

Blessed
is the spot,
and the house, and the place,
and the city, and the heart,
and the mountain, and the refuge,
and the cave, and the valley,
and the land, and the sea,
and the island, and the meadow
where mention of
God
hath been made,
and His praise
glorified.

Baha'i

(How to Make Space Around You)

Pick a crowd you would like to thin,
Stretch out your arms
and spin.

In moments of extreme despair,
crouch and gradually rise
to clear a column in the air.

If the crowd is slow in thinning,
keep spinning.

ANNE SPENCER LINDBERGH

ROBIN'S SONG

God bless the field and bless the furrow,
   Stream and branch and rabbit burrow,
Hill and stone and flower and tree,
   From Bristol Town to Wetherby—
Bless the sun and bless the sleet,
   Bless the lane and bless the street.
Bless the night and bless the day,
   From Somerset and all the way
   To the meadows of Cathay;
Bless the minnow, bless the whale,
   Bless the rainbow and the hail,
Bless the nest and bless the leaf,
   Bless the righteous and the thief,
Bless the wing and bless the fin,
   Bless the air I travel in,
Bless the mill and bless the mouse,
   Bless the miller's bricken house,
Bless the earth and bless the sea,
   God bless you and God bless me!

Old English

40

There, where the skylark's
singing crosses the cuckoo's
dark song, there am I.

KYORAI

Deep peace of the running wave to you,
Deep peace of the flowing air to you,
Deep peace of the quiet earth to you,
Deep peace of the shining stars to you,
Deep peace of the Son of Peace to you.
Amen.

Gaelic

41

For the Earth

illustrated by CHRISTINE DAVENIER

Even the seasons form a great circle in their changing,
and always come back again to where they were

GLORIA

The whole world is full of glory.

Here is the glory of created things,
   the earth and the sky,
   the sun and the moon,
   the stars and the vast expanses:

Here is fellowship
   with all that was created,
   the air and the wind,
   cloud and rain,
   sunshine and snow:

All life like the bubbling of a flowing river
   and the dark currents of the depths of the sea
   is full of glory.

EUROS BOWEN

The blowing wind,
   the mild, moist air,
   the exquisite greening
   of trees and grasses—

In their beginning,
   in their ending,
   they give God their praise.

HILDEGARD OF BINGEN

Who has made the earth?
   Oh, who has made the cows?
Thakur made the earth.
   Thakur made the cows.

Santal

Prayer to the Mountain Spirit

Lord of the Mountain,
Reared within the Mountain,
Young Man, Chieftain,
Hear a young man's prayer!
Hear a prayer for cleanness.
Keeper of the strong rain,
Drumming on the Mountain;
Lord of the small rain
That restores the earth in newness;
Keeper of the clean rain,
Hear a prayer for wholeness.

Young Man, Chieftain,
Hear a prayer for fleetness.
Keeper of the deer's way,
Reared among the eagles,
Clear my feet of slothness.
Keeper of the paths of men,
Hear a prayer for straightness.

Hear a prayer for courage.
Lord of the thin peaks,
Reared amid the thunders;
Keeper of the headlands
Holding up the harvest,
Keeper of the strong rocks,
Hear a prayer for staunchness.

Young Man, Chieftain,
Spirit of the Mountain!

Navajo

47

HOMAGE TO GOD

I have seen the waters flow in the river.
I have seen the flowers along the banks of the river.
Passing by, I have gazed upon the countryside
And inhaled the perfume of the orange blossoms.
I have been grateful to God and I have said thank you to him.

Algerian

THE PRAYER
OF THE LITTLE DUCKS

Dear God,
give us a flood of water.
Let it rain tomorrow and always.
Give us plenty of little slugs
and other luscious things to eat.
Protect all folk who quack
and everyone who knows how to swim.
Amen.

CARMEN BERNOS DE GASZTOLD

HURT NO LIVING THING

Hurt no living thing;
   Ladybird, nor butterfly,
   Nor moth with dusty wing,
Nor cricket chirping cheerily,
Nor grasshopper so light of leap,
   Nor dancing gnat, nor beetle fat,
   Nor harmless worms that creep.

CHRISTINA ROSSETTI

I believe a leaf of grass is no less
    than the journey-work of the stars . . .
And the running blackberry would adorn
    the parlors of heaven.
And the narrowest hinge in my hand
    puts to scorn all machinery,
And the cow crunching with depressed head
    surpasses any statue,
And a mouse is miracle enough
    to stagger sextillions of infidels!

WALT WHITMAN
from LEAVES OF GRASS

This earth . . .
I never damage,
I look after.
Fire is nothing,
just clean up.
When you burn,
New grass coming up.
That mean good animal soon . . .
might be goose, long-neck turtle,
    goanna, possum.
Burn him off . . .
new grass coming up,
new life all over.

BILL NEIDJIE

50

Everything the Power of the World does is done in a circle. The sky is round, and I have heard that the earth is round like a ball, and so are all the stars. The wind, in its greatest power, whirls. Birds make their nests in circles, for theirs is the same religion as ours. The sun comes forth and goes down again in a circle. The moon does the same, and both are round.

Even the seasons form a great circle in their changing, and always come back again to where they were. The life of a man is a circle from childhood to childhood, and so it is in everything where power moves.

Black Elk

Let me come with these donkeys, Lord, into your land,
These beasts who bow their heads so gently, and stand
With their small feet joined together in a fashion
Utterly gentle, asking your compassion.

FRANCIS JAMMES
from "A Prayer to Go to Paradise with the Donkeys"

52

Flying out from
the Great Buddha's nose:
a swallow.

ISSA

Crowned crane
Beautiful crowned crane of power
Bird of the word
Your voice took part in creation;
You the drum and the stick that beats it
What you speak is spoken clearly
Ancestor of praise-singers, even the tree
Upon which you perch is worthy of commendation
Speaking of birds, you make the list complete
Some have big heads and small beaks
Others have big beaks and small heads
But you have self-knowledge;
It is the Creator himself who has adorned you!

Bamana
from "Crowned Crane"

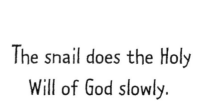

Feeding the birds
is also a form of prayer . . .

POPE PIUS XII

The snail does the Holy
Will of God slowly.

G. K. CHESTERTON

PIED BEAUTY

Glory be to God for dappled things—
   For skies of couple-color as a brinded cow;
     For rose-moles all in stipple upon trout that swim;
Fresh-firecoal chestnut-falls; finches' wings;
   Landscape plotted and pieced—fold, fallow, and plow;
     And all trades, their gear and tackle and trim.
All things counter, original, spare, strange;
   Whatever is fickle, freckled (who knows how?)
     With swift, slow; sweet, sour; adazzle, dim;
He fathers-forth whose beauty is past change:
   Praise Him.

GERARD MANLEY HOPKINS

54

All you big things, bless the Lord
Mount Kilimanjaro and Lake Victoria
The Rift Valley and the Serengeti Plain
Fat baobabs and shady mango trees
All eucalyptus and tamarind trees
Bless the Lord
Praise and extol Him for ever and ever.

All you tiny things, bless the Lord
Busy black ants and hopping fleas
Wriggling tadpoles and mosquito larvae
Flying locusts and water drops
Pollen dust and tsetse flies
Millet seeds and dried dagaa
Bless the Lord
Praise and extol Him for ever and ever.

East African

55

ON MORNING WINGS, IN OCEANS DEEP

Lord, you look at me and know me,
Every step I take, you show me.

When I rise, and when I rest,
You will always know me best.

Where I walk, or sit, or stand,
You still hold me in your hand.

And if I don't know how to pray,
You understand me, anyway.

Once when I was lost, you found me.
Then I felt your arms around me.

When I'm afraid and want to hide,
You are always by my side.

When I'm lonely, you are near,
When I'm angry, you stay here,

High as heaven bright, you greet me,
Down in darkness, too, you meet me.

You are with me everywhere:
In light and shadow, fire and air;

In every tiny grain of sand;
And in the desert, vast and grand;

On morning wings, in oceans deep;
When I'm awake, and when I sleep.

In my secret self, you made me,
In the blazing sun, you shade me.

Know me, lead me, guide my way
Through every hour of every day,

For all my life, in all I do,
Let me always be with you.

REEVE LINDBERGH
based on Psalm 139

For the Night

illustrated by ANITA JERAM

Toward me the darkness comes rustling

I will lift up mine eyes unto the hills,
from whence cometh my help.
My help cometh from the Lord,
which made heaven and earth.

He will not suffer thy foot to be moved:
he that keepeth thee will not slumber.
Behold, he that keepeth Israel
shall neither slumber nor sleep.

The Lord is thy keeper:
the Lord is thy shade upon thy right hand.
The sun shall not smite thee by day,
nor the moon by night.

The Lord shall preserve thee from all evil:
he shall preserve thy soul.
The Lord shall preserve
thy going out and thy coming in,
from this time forth,
and even for evermore.

Psalm 121

60

O God,
Make us children of quietness
and heirs of peace.
Amen.

SAINT CLEMENT

I feel the suffering of millions.
And yet, when I look up at the sky,
I somehow feel that everything will change
for the better, that this cruelty too
will end, that peace and tranquility
will return once more.

ANNE FRANK

Downy white feathers
are moving beneath the sunset
and along the edge of the world.

Papago

The sun is slowly departing,
It is slower in its setting;
Black bats will be swooping when the sun is gone,
That is all.

The spirit children are beneath,
They are moving back and forth;
They roll in play among tufts of white eagle down,
That is all.

Papago

In the great night my heart will go out;
Toward me the darkness comes rustling.
In the great night my heart will go out.

Papago

May there be peace in the higher regions;
may there be peace in the firmament;
may there be peace on earth.
May the waters flow peacefully;
may the herbs and plants grow peacefully;
may all the divine powers bring unto us peace.
The supreme Lord is peace.
May we all be in peace, peace, and only peace;
and may that peace come unto each of us.

SHANTI—SHANTI—SHANTI!

from the VEDAS

Now that the sun has set,
I sit and rest, and think of you.
Give my weary body peace.
Let my legs and arms stop aching,
Let my nose stop sneezing,
Let my head stop thinking.
Let me sleep in your arms.

Dinka

THE RAIN AT NIGHT

The good rain knows when to fall,
Coming in this spring to help the seeds,
Choosing to fall by night
    with a friendly wind,
Silently moistening the whole earth.
Over this silent wilderness
    the clouds are dark.
The only light shines from a river boat.
Tomorrow morning everything
    will be red and wet,
And all Chengtu will be covered
    with blossoming flowers.

Tu Fu

Even when the gates of heaven
are shut to prayer,
they are open to tears.

from the TALMUD

I believe in the sun
    even when it is not shining.
I believe in love
    even when feeling it not.
I believe in God
    even when He is silent.

Jewish

We are the stars which sing.
  We sing with our light.
  We are the birds of fire.
  We fly over the sky.
  Our light is a voice.
  We make a road
  For the spirit to pass over.

Passamaquoddy

The moon and the year
  travel and pass away:
  also the day, also the wind.
Also the flesh passes away
  to the place of its quietness.

Mayan

There are stars up above,
    so far away we only see their light long,
    long after the star itself is gone.
And so it is with people that we loved.
Their memories keep shining
    ever brightly
    though their time with us is done.
But the stars that light up the darkest night,
    these are the stars that guide us.
As we live our days these are the ways we remember,
    we remember.
As we live our days these days we remember,
    we remember.

Jewish

Lord, let Your light be only for the day,
   And the darkness for the night.
   And let my dress, my poor humble dress
   Lie quietly over my chair at night.

Let the church-bells be silent,
   My neighbor Ivan not ring them at night.
   Let the wind not waken the children
   Out of their sleep at night.

Let the hen sleep on its roost, the horse in the stable
   All through the night.
   Remove the stone from the middle of the road
   That the thief may not stumble at night.

Let heaven be quiet during the night.
   Restrain the lightning, silence the thunder.
   They should not frighten mothers giving birth
   To their babies at night.

And me too protect against fire and water,
   Protect my poor roof at night.
   Let my dress, my poor humble dress
   Lie quietly over my chair at night.

NATHAN BOMZE

Our Father, who art in heaven,
Hallowed be thy name.
Thy kingdom come.
Thy will be done,
On earth, as it is in heaven.
Give us this day our daily bread.
And forgive us our trespasses,
As we forgive those
    who trespass against us.
And lead us not into temptation,
But deliver us from evil.
For thine is the kingdom,
    and the power, and the glory,
    for ever and ever.
Amen.

from the Gospel of Matthew

May every creature
    abound in well-being and peace.

May every living being,
    weak or strong, the long and the small,
    the short and the medium-sized,
    the mean and the great,

May every living creature,
    seen and unseen
    those dwelling far off,
    those wanting to be born,

May all attain peace.

Buddhist

O heavenly Father, protect and bless
all things that have breath:
guard them from all evil
and let them sleep in peace.

ALBERT SCHWEITZER

Good night! Good night!
Far flies the light;
But still God's love
Shall shine above,
Making all bright,
Good night! Good night!

VICTOR HUGO

Index of first lines

Acknowledgments

For the Day

"I am like a bear . . ." from *American Indian Poetry*, George W. Cronyn, Ed. Copyright © 1918, copyright renewed © 1962 by George W. Cronyn. Reprinted by permission of Ballantine Books, a division of Random House Inc.

"May the Lord bless you and protect you . . ." (THE THREEFOLD BLESSING) from *Mahzor Hadash* revised and expanded edition, compiled and edited by Rabbi Sidney Greenburg and Jonathan D. Levine. Reprinted by permission of the Prayer Book Press, Inc.

"Oh God, give me, I pray Thee . . ." by Muhammed from *The Little Book of Prayers*. Copyright © 1996 by David Schiller. Reprinted by permission of Workman Publishing Co., Inc. New York. All rights reserved.

"Do harm to nobody . . ." by Abdu'l-Bahá. Reprinted by permission of the Bahá'í Publishing Trust.

"O Lord, My God . . ." (EILI, EILI) by Hannah Senesh from *The Family Treasury of Jewish Holidays* by Malka Drucker. Reprinted by permission of Little Brown & Co.

"Master of the Universe . . ." (GRANT ME THE ABILITY TO BE ALONE) by Rabbi Nachman of Bratslav from *The Family Treasury of Jewish Holidays* by Malka Drucker. Reprinted by permission of Little Brown & Co.

"Turn . . . ," excerpt from WHY HAST THOU? by Guru Nanak, A.D. 1469–1538, translated by Teja Singh from *Lamps of Fire: The Spirit of Religions*. Selection copyright © 1958 by Juan Mascaró. Published by Methuen Books, 1961. Reprinted by permission of Kathleen Mascaró.

"The flute of the Infinite . . ." by Kabir, translated by Rabindranath Tagore from *Lamps of Fire: The Spirit of Religions*. Selection copyright © 1958 by Juan Mascaró. Published by Methuen Books, 1961. Reprinted by permission of Visva-Bharati University (Publishing Department), Calcutta, India.

THE CIRCLE OF DAYS by Reeve Lindbergh. Copyright © 1999 by Reeve Lindbergh. Reprinted by permission of the Rhoda Weyr Agency, New York.

"There is a Light that shines . . . ," excerpt from the CHANDOGYA UPANISHAD, translated by Juan Mascaró from *The Himalayas of the Soul* in the Wisdom of the East series. Reprinted by permission of John Murray (Publishers) Ltd.

"May the sun rise well . . . ," excerpt from SONG FOR FAIR WEATHER, from *American Indian Poetry*, George W. Cronyn, Ed. Copyright © 1918, copyright renewed © 1962 by George W. Cronyn. Reprinted by permission of Ballantine Books, a division of Random House Inc.

"By day the sun shines . . . ," excerpt from the *Dhammapada*, translated by Juan Mascaró. Penguin Classics, 1973. Copyright © 1973 by Juan Mascaró. Reprinted by permission of Penguin Books Ltd.

For the Home

"God bless the master of this house . . ." (WASSAIL SONG) reprinted with permission of Simon & Schuster, Inc. from *Fireside Book of Folksongs* by Margaret Bradford Boni. Copyright © 1947, copyright renewed © 1974 by Simon & Schuster, Inc.

"If in your heart you make . . ." (IT DEPENDS ON YOU) by Angelus Silesius from *The Enlightened Heart* by Stephen Mitchell. Copyright © 1989 by Stephen Mitchell. Reprinted by permission of HarperCollins Publishers, New York.

"See the world as your self . . ." by Lao-tzu from *Tao Te Ching: a New English Version: with foreword and notes by Stephen Mitchell*. Translation copyright © 1988 by Stephen Mitchell. Reprinted by permission of HarperCollins Publishers, New York.

"May it be delightful my house . . ." translated by John Bierhorst from *In the Trail of the Wind: American Indian Poems and Ritual Orations*, John Bierhorst, Ed. Reprinted by permission of Farrar, Straus & Giroux, Inc.

BREAD by Freda Elton Young from *Book of a Thousand Poems*. Published by Unwin Hyman Ltd. Reprinted by permission of HarperCollins Publishers Ltd., London.

MOTHER OF BROWN-NESS by Margaret Walker from *Soul Looks Back in Wonder* by Tom Feelings. Copyright © 1993 by Tom Feelings. Reprinted by permission of Dial Books for Young Readers, a division of Penguin Putnam Inc.

"The lands around my dwelling . . ." translated by John Bierhorst from *In the Trail of the Wind: American Indian Poems and Ritual Orations*, John Bierhorst, Ed. Reprinted by permission of Farrar, Straus & Giroux, Inc.

ALONE by Budger Davison from *Spirit Song: A Collection of Aboriginal Poetry* compiled by Lorraine Mafi-Williams, 1993, Omnibus Books, Australia.

"Blessed is the spot . . . ," Bahá'í prayer. Reprinted by kind permission of the Bahá'í Publishing Trust.

(HOW TO MAKE SPACE AROUND YOU) by Anne Spencer Lindbergh. Copyright © by Anne Spencer Lindbergh. Reprinted by permission of Reeve Lindbergh.

ROBIN'S SONG from *Book of a Thousand Poems*, Bell & Hyman, 1983. Reprinted by permission of HarperCollins Publishers Ltd., London.

"There, where the skylark's singing . . ." (THERE AM I) by Kyorai from *More Cricket Songs: Japanese haiku*, translated by Harry Behn. Copyright © 1971 by Harry Behn. Copyright © renewed 1999 by Prescott Behn, Pamela Behn Adam, and Peter Behn. Reprinted by permission of Marian Reiner.

"Deep peace of the running wave to you . . ." (INVOCATION OF PEACE) from *Book of a Thousand Poems*, Bell & Hyman, 1983. Reprinted by permission of HarperCollins Publishers Ltd., London.